C000173531

VALERIE WOHLFELD

Woman
with Wing
Removed

Truman State University Press
New Odyssey Series

Copyright © 2010 Valerie Wohlfeld
All rights reserved
tsup.truman.edu

Cover art: Winged Nike of Samothrace, Parian marble, ca. 190 BCE? Found in Samothrace in 1863. Louvre, Paris. Photo © Marie-Lan Nguyen/Wikimedia Commons.

Cover design: Teresa Wheeler
Type: Minion Pro © Adobe Systems Inc.
Printed by: Thomson-Shore, Dexter, Michigan USA

Library of Congress Cataloging-in-Publication Data
Wohlfeld, Valerie, 1956–
   Woman with wing removed : poems / by Valerie Wohlfeld.
      p. cm. — (New odyssey series)
   ISBN 978-1-935503-06-4 (pbk. : alk. paper)
   I. Title.
   PS3573.O394W66 2010
   811'.54—dc22
                                                              2010006353

No part of this work may be reproduced or transmitted in any format by any means without written permission from the publisher.

The paper in this publication meets or exceeds the minimum requirements of the American National Standard for Information Sciences—Permanence of Paper for Printed Library Materials, ANSI Z39.48–1992.

Woman With Wing Removed

For my mother

Thou art thy mother's glass, and she in thee
Calls back the lovely April of her prime
                                    —William Shakespeare

Contents

Acknowledgments

Grateful acknowledgment is made to the following publications for work, some under different titles, that first appeared in them.

Antioch Review: "Nautilus"
Arion: A Journal of Humanities and the Classics: "Persephone Writes Home (Parts 2, 3)"
Christianity and Literature: "Apples"
The Classical Outlook Journal of the American Classical League: "Echo," "Persephone Writes Home (Part 1)"
Ellipsis Magazine: "Dust out of Eden"
The Endicott Review: "Letter"
First Things: "Walking the Sea"
Free Inquiry: "Birds of the New World"
The Hopkins Review: "Gift," "My Father's World"
Journal of the American Medical Association: "Déjà vu," "Vertigo"
Louisiana Literature: "Cat and Cuckoo," "Woman with Wing Removed"
Luna: "I in Eden Born"
The Lyric: "Salt"
Midstream: "Veined-Garden"
The New Criterion: "Vessel"
New England Review: "Hawk," "Pears"
North American Review: "Violin"
North Dakota Quarterly: "Obiter Dicta"
Pinyon: "Agave"
Ploughshares: "Poppies"
Prairie Schooner: "Fire and Flux"
Seneca Review: "Apple"
Sou'wester: "Feral," "Horoscope"
Valparaiso Poetry Review: "Wedding Portrait"
The Wallace Stevens Journal: "The Living Page"
The Yale Review: "Envy"

"Handkerchief" appeared in the anthology *Against Agamemnon: War Poetry* (edited by James Adams, WaterWood Press).

"Veined-Garden" appeared in the anthology *Best Jewish Writing 2003* (edited by Arthur Kurzweil, Wiley and Sons Publishers).

"Apple," "Fire and Flux," and "Nautilus" appeared in the anthology *Under the Rock Umbrella: Modern American Poets from 1951 to 1976* (edited by William Walsh, Mercer University Press).

Part One

Envy

I envy the hawk her eye,
that culls the hare and the quail from their nests.
She honors the Bible, an eye for an eye,
and expels in the pellet's feathers and bone what she cannot digest.

She knows the wind before the wind knows itself.
She flies the valley blind in her mind while on the perch of her captor.
The quarry's shin of butcher beef she claims for herself.
With bells of brass nickel, each leg strapped,

she cannot untie the falconer's knot.
The smell of the glove is rank with blood
and mauled of its leather stitches by dogs and rats. Rot
excites her and she waits for the lifting of the hood

as if a bride under a lace veil longing to sigh
at the crush of the groom's hands. I envy the hawk her eye.

Wasp Nest

Hanging heart of papier-mâché.
Web and womb and watchtower
of cellulose and saliva. Sway
of the piñata dented and clubbed in its hour.
Hum and hub
of a city created cell by cell.
Sour layered linen of a Pharaoh's tomb.
Citadel and motel
casting the queen out before
the killing frost. To digest the living spider, to eat
it as the larvae do! Corridor by corridor,
slung suite to suite for one bittersweet
season, then the wasps are dead. One year
hangs the fragile house, then the empire is over.

4

Pears

This terminus an epilogue of consummation.
Like the slaughterhouse heart done of bone!
Core of seeds like a spine forced open.
Tempered twist of swollen hip overthrown

by the discord of rot and perfume.
Seed instructs the deconstructed flesh.
What morning news is not old by afternoon?
Even the sleeping god in the crèche

comes and goes season by season like the bee
leasing the rooming cells wallpapered
neighbor by neighbor: who is not queen is refugee.
In the glass hive each bee has its bed.

The fall of pears is like the fall of the queen:
her fragrance holds the tribe together at the murder scene.

Nautilus

Snood of chignon, invisibly-staked French Twist,
little platinum bun of the nautilus shell.
Mollusk, architect dictating a nunnery:
vault built after mantled vault,
pristine coil upon coil, every door
without passage in or out, sealed
against lover, bridegroom, gigolo,
the father who is not Father.
In sterile-threaded stitches
surgeon suturing shut the missing eye
closed against the brutal face.
Every wall thin as bridal veil,
fragile-pored as osteoporotic bone;
white-washed as finials,
frescoed plasters awaiting limed colors,
inner watery white of pith or marrow.
And in that nunnery silence distilled
into matins, sext, vespers—
with chants and bells, singings and meditations,
all the prayers of shipwreck sent there by the sea.

Refrain

Tired of the crows, I turned to the marsh geese
and the blue heron that stood
on one leg as balanced as the clef in the crease
of the staff. Geese, brushed blue, were on the Wedgwood

too. Tired of the crows I turned to the cry
of the unmated purple martin—my love
had built a house for the martin's mate to lie
in, just as I had the arms of my love

to rest on. Still the martin's mate did not come
to the beautiful box or the hanging feeder's seed.
Like the cardinals my love wore red and I wore brown;
I was in crushed velvet and my lover in tweed.

I turned back to the crows; their thundered refrain,
and I not knowing who was kin—my lover or the rain.

Love Letters

Fire in a clasp at my throat: the silk scarf's red
rose—and roses rare in winter! For thirty years
your love letters hidden: how dead
the yellow and gray paper and the little smear

of the ink in the sabotage of a tear.
Crowned in a scaffold of buds and briar,
the rose on its black silk square. How clear,
memory, like the drama of death in amber.

In some theater of light-years, in some distant
planet, we are together and the rose is new again;
and God is not old but is writing the commandments
and creating his world of gravity and sin.

But now the rose is like fire and the letters tinder
to hold in arthritic hands turned tender.

Salt

Teaspoon by teaspoon the sea fills
the little twin halves of my locket.
The last of the wheat falls to the winterkill
and the sea turns to salt in my pocket.

Banded as madras, the sea goes on.
The rendezvous of blue meets blue.
Out of the arctic, white gulls go on
colonizing hemispheres. The sea and the skull sew

themselves shut in death's masts and sheets, sails and sirens,
buntings and spindrift. The dead's bloat as endnote.
The sea reinvents itself again as each wren
invents flight. Midas turned mud to gold and rewrote

the March light. Finger of salt I pull
over my mother, salt my mother pulls over me. Grave rocks cradle.

Walking the Sea

Walking the sea, I think of the small diaspora
of the hermit crab, and the unshackled shell.
I think of the sealed spiral, niche and cupola
the nautilus crafts as if the ether-windowed spirit-level.
I think of the mollusk that lets the coffined pearl,
blind eye white as albumen—grow.

Walking the sea, I think of the skull, and the curl
of organs in the canopic jar: glassy vertigo,
staring-in, stares back, the afterlife or another death.
Walking the sea I see in the ropey egg cases
the umbilical cord's birthed death; my little faulty breath
that displaces my mother's linked necklaces

of veins and blood. Vowels I cannot swallow,
I hear again in my first word, *mama*—all the diasporas to follow.

The Living Page

"Death is the mother of beauty"
—Wallace Stevens

Death is the mother of beauty:
perhaps the lawyer found a small dead beetle
or the rattled tattle-tell tail of the bookworm

turning out the carcass of the living page. Did he see
death and beauty on a lady's handkerchief settle
inside the drawer beside beetle and tome? To mother beauty

out of death, the perfumed linen is the very
scent of death. If the Hawaiian white ginger fell,
pressed flower, out of the law book: or, the trail of the bookworm

led back to the hibiscus and jasmine, meeting destiny
preserved inside his great books of law; and the shell
left empty at the shore. *Death is the mother of beauty,*

of the little beetle in the narrow drawer. Plea
of his wife to make love and the look of ecstasy
nearly the look of death's eyes as the bookworm's

rattle falls quiet. He understood measure, iambics, repartee,
recursion and cadence. To make love to make death to make beauty:
his honeymoon conceived that *death is the mother of beauty;*
beside the Floridian blooms, still the rattled tail of the bookworm.

Fiddlehead Fern

Ringed eye of the peacock's hundred eyes.
Patina of bronzes shipwrecked.
Laced eyelet, scraps the seamstress prizes,
ribbons rolled tight, raveled edges to collect.

Coiled craft, springs, gear, watch
without tell-tale hands or batteries.
Tightest porthole without a latch.
Round coin for Charon and death's ease.

Wayward hair tucked around a tendriled bun.
Size of a newborn's fist clenched tight.
All of life lived between the muck and the sun.
Little green womb fertile as Aphrodite.

In late spring the stem sways;
already the spiral knot begins to fray.

Herb Vinegar

Tarragon stalks and strings,
furled-out strands and spikes
of rosemary at the watery reaches of the opening
jar. Branching greens like

ships mysteriously settled in bottled glass.
Some final growth ruined to runt
like a specimen's dwarfed mass
drowned in a little forest's stunted

platter of bonsai. Ocean without wave
and still the tormented curves of stem
formed as from some sea-saved
voyage. Preserved stratagem

of the Pharaoh: first death in the sour linen;
second death awakens the flowering cassia again.

Poppies

Clashing paper umbrellas of red
and orange. The fur of the moth's eye-
spot centered: wind shakes the poppy, and the poppy shakes the head
of the pod shapely as Egyptian skull, bone-dry.

Spliced spore, sap and milk: tiny black seeds
seamed inside; like the pocket walls' little wooden veins
holding the paper umbrellas up. Every cocktail cherry bleeds,
stemmed, swirled, colors real as unreal rains

glassed in grenadine. Drowned pulp, poppy petals
never color-fast; meant for show: quickly red
abandons the poppy, and the flesh mummifies the shell's
seeded Pharaonic head. The living, the dead,

grow side by side in every soil-bed. Breath comes cheap
to Morpheus as to the ancient poppies' silent shackled sleep.

Morpheus

I have a fetal need for mothering night;
the runic bloom the poppies lose in fall;
the jellyfish's sting and kiss; the blanched white
sky of stars and the eyeball

spun to shuttered dark. In sleep
I feel the broken fingers of the starfish
climb my ebony bed, and the deep
sea slugs trail like a liquid ghost their wish

to be the lips' sensuous ruse of susurrus.
Is sleep madness without cause,
yet the cure for madness, sleep? The noose
adjusts itself to let life pause—

I am febrile and contrite:
let come my mothering night.

Scar

Closed slipknot that chose
to end in its own beginning. Limestone for the fern
to live on. Graft that grows
in the foreign stem. Spot of ash in the urn.

Vermeil, bronze or silver tulle,
pearlescent marbled whorl,
spiral-bound ammonite fossil,
chevron from some ancient war.

Single pearl earring the clasp has left.
Wax cast out of the mold.
Seam of the fetus at chin and palate.
Soul mate to the mar of the mole.

Line where glaze meets glaze, the fired china
bears the mutant colors of the kiln's patina.

Between Asp and Web

In hierarchies of love, draw down the firefly!—
and let the spider move in. Birthed
anarchies of dust are the stars' alibi.
How angels and priests share the narrow berth

with the chorus in the pews of heaven.
Already the world, saved from chaos,
is falling back to chaos. Leaven
sweetens the bread but the cosmos

is not changed by sweet or sour.
The galaxy travels through gravity
while we connect the dots of the firefly and the flower.
The church spider weaves point a to point b;

ab to bc, the silk-staged strands between the asp
and the web. How different, the spinning spider, to the hung wasp!

Shekinah

The Shekinah is held by many to represent
the feminine attributes of the presence of God.

God and I are like the braid
half-wild in a horse's mane; the love-knot
in the ring of gold; the ivory and the jade

(so cold to touch!) in the inlaid
jewelry. It took the both of us to turn Lot's
wife to salt. God and I are like the braid:

the parted hair in equal measure, precisely made.
I am the rain and snow of God who's got
a myriad of moods beneath his gold and ivory, and the jade

the pagans use in the statues that they trade.
I am the lovesick face of Shabbat:
God and I are like the braid

the matron and the virgin, the nursemaid and the barmaid,
finally let down. It is I who helped David with the slingshot.
Each knuckle holds my different rings of gold, ivory, and jade.

I am rain and snow and the soil not spared by the spade;
in every womb I grow clot by clot.
God and I are like the braid
in the ring of gold, the carven ivory and the chilly jade.

Part Two

Letter

Upstairs, I write the letter I will not send to you.
Downstairs, you sit between summoned hum and screen.
Upstairs, envelopes adhere in bitter glue.

Alphabet stolen from the Etruscans, your typed rendezvous
with the kind of girl who started ancient Grecian schemes.
Archaic ink! Upstairs I review the letter never sent to you.

Upstairs, we start the pills we take to stop the blues.
Morning is routine: downstairs, caffeine;
upstairs, the little amber tear sets the mucilage glue.

I read the letter until it seems like déjà vu;
our gold-stamped monogram the go-between
of pages seen, unseen, and never sent downstairs to you.

Could I live in the flickered mien and light that's new?
Blue hum: smoke screen for the *deus ex machina?*
Upstairs, blotted ink is obsolete. The fountain pen belonged to you.

Once, men held love abstract from view.
Once, women knew if love was true, or might have been.
Upstairs, creases align a letter never sent to you.
Upstairs, lit sealing wax bites bitter glue.

Vertigo

The heart near perishes in the chambers of the blood
that set it free to beat minute by minute:
little miracle of valve and flap and in gravity the circled flood
of backwards blood again, and the heady rein and bit

that harness auricle to auricle. Ecstatic
static, the electricity switches on
the stubborn tics the body stutters on. Knife-nicked
the shackled stasis of the fat-marbled meat hung on

the butcher's hook: once the blood
ran its sprints and marathons to no ribboned
finish line. The heart lives in the corridors of the blood
where dutiful it feeds the sudden-summoned

vein. In those sounded veins the hollow echoes
of a chambered hall where sits Cerberus eyeing all of hell in vertigo.

Déjà Vu

My heart is out of true. No plumb line,
no chalk mark, guides the scribbled line
aligned on valve and wall. What architect
drew the hollow vein? Obsidian knife and Aztec
slew the primal blood. Jerry-built and askew,
                my heart is out of true.

The plumb line is dead-reckoned. Savant:
the auricle's second, the pump clairvoyant;
in half-time beats does a lifetime pass.
Breath, like sands, lasso the hourglass.
Does the circulating blood perceive its déjà vu?
                My heart is out of true.

Silent-Seized

Bring me the ice pack, I wish to freeze
my heart, embalm the great aorta,
forked branch that is all effort
and squeeze of blood that runs until it silent-seizes.
Sawed-through the breastbone, the brutal striptease
on the operating table, which is the surgeon's sport.
The beautiful blood the color of port, and the spout's
spilled murmured wheeze drains dry to ease

life back to the split and splinted heart.
How much I might prefer the slap
of cold blood's slush, sluicing in the sting and smart
of captive veins that drain and abort the blood
in and out the flaps and valves and the wiretap
of the measured pulse. Freeze me fast or bury me in sod!

Paper Clock Kit

A clock of paper pinions and axles assembled in the space age!
The lightest of pendulums to swing.
With X-Acto knives we mutilate the page.
The seams, the hinge, the spring,

the little teeth that lock, the tabs to fold
marked *a–z,* the line of glue to squeeze and hold
the paper wheel: we build the scaffold
of 200 pieces to make a ticking whole.

If only a paper heart could be so precisely made.
To hold the dry shudder of a bloodless model.
If the heart too had escapement and anchor—would it feel jaded
at the pulse, without the cell to beat inside the paper shell?

We sit with scissors, knife, and glue;
we will put the clock together but not the heart's disjointed tissue.

If Only

If only you were the asp and I
Cleopatra! In the ruin
of the tepid, dry snakeskin I
would wrap myself from shank to shin.

How beautiful the scales on your back!
How deadly your occult poison.
How languorous your slow flow of blood in attack.
How precise each fang, how without noise

the fatal bite. Your length tangles my limbs
and I give myself over to your coils, I let
you hold my limp body quiet as lovers. Our dim
dull blood stills in mingled duet.

Let me count the hundreds of bones that let
your backbone slither and arch, before the poison sets.

Feral

Let my heart draw the bees like a tent of honey!
Let flame the savage stain of scavenged sumac
in my veins. Let wolves and frenzy instruct me.
After the wolves, let the crows come in their black clique.

Lodged loam of comb, my heart is honey without sting.
Like the crow I drink out of the farmer's well;
meadows and forests all pass by in my wing's
shadow. In the beekeeper's smoke, I do not let my heart quell.

Let the wolf build her den in my heart;
her blind litter lingers and is my own bloodline.
I hunt the snake, I feed on the corn, it is my art.
Hummed havoc of bees, the feral whine—

let my heart not quiet, not quit,
heart pieced and pierced in flesh like the fruit's bitter pit.

Daybreak

Love is the wick untrimmed, the threaded fire,
the braided cotton cordoned in the melted wax.
Love is the blood held at bay in wars, the cease-fire
and the sudden drums all quiet, and then the little climax

of the climbing sun at daybreak. Always
it is daybreak to the heart that knows no night.
Love is the flag with the bullet hole and fray.
Love is not the kite but the kite's

little tails that fly behind it. And the wind,
the desolate wind that moves the kite across
the sky cannot help itself, cannot rescind
the turbulent eddies and the pathos

the great inanimate tides of air
must feel—that love is only another name of despair.

Cat and Cuckoo

You have left me alone with the cat
and the cuckoo clock. From Germany
a distant relative sent the clock over. In the slats
of the dark little house the cuckoo is never free,

the plank-carved wings never fly,
and the horrible chime imitating his song
makes even the cat in her sly silent way prophesy
that the old world is gone, and the new world is wrong.

I sit between the cat and the cuckoo,
we three are not quite adversaries, friends, or heroes:
I feel flawed and ornate like the bird on its floe of faux bamboo;
the cat is too aloof and the cuckoo too slow.

You left. There is a grief here—do you care?—
it is like putting the tortoise shell comb of another,
                              already dead, into my own hair.

Anthracite

You are away. I sit on the couch by day
and your cat sleeps on my bed at night.
On one side of the window the cat sits and the jay
sits on the other side. From some great height,

in a city's skyscraper, you sip café au lait
out of a white porcelain mug. You might
or might not think of me. The hotel foyer
with its suitcases, busboys, and mirrors is too bright

and you think of the house you have not seen since Friday.
How can I tell you I am not quite all right,
like the cat I am on one side of the glass, like the jay
you are on another side? How beautiful is the anthracite

in a box filled with your collection of minerals. Tight
in one hand I hold the dark stone. In the other hand only sunlight.

Rime

In a box is my wedding dress
crushed in its veil. Twenty-seven years
ago I wore its hundred pleats and laces. Like chess
we move and strategize; like the auctioneer　·

we box our possessions for the bidder;
like a foreign war we cross and re-cross the ocean;
like some unanswerable riddle we consider and reconsider.
All our peccadilloes are our potent potion—

we survive like the tulle across my face
those twenty-seven years ago, in cross-hatched shadow.
There is no fall from grace, and yet the papers in your briefcase
await the signing and my initials. There is still time under the
　　mistletoe

to kiss—let us kiss before the season passes:
the window in rime and the candles sunk into the brass.

Bride

My mother covered the mirrors for mourning
the day I was married. My husband
had me cut off my long braid that same morning.
Taken from my sister's closet, my wedding dress was secondhand.

How difficult it is to love him now
that my hair is short. He used to wish
my hair to grow so long it caught in my bangles! My vows
hold me to him, but my dreams are selfish:

I want to give my sister back our wedding dress,
with the tiny waist I had to let the seams out
of, so the double row of pearl buttons would not press
and pinch my skin. Like the spring drought

I feel parched and old without my mother;
I long to pull off the cloth from her mirrors.

Violin

I am like the violin no one plays. In the attic
the wood grain's varnish and veneer
lie with the other mistakes: the batik
banner, the beetle-eaten head of the mounted deer,

the stained cashmere sweater, and the odd love letter
not set on fire. Once you cradled the hourglass
figure, tucked in your chin, and fingered the strings without regret.
The embossed pebbled leather case with brass

hinges is lost; once you carried it back and forth
on the subway and played in the underground stations.
You rode from south to north, your music's worth
of coins thrown into the open case. The attic sun

and the unsung music cannot startle the dust and decay.
I am like the violin no one plays.

Moroccan Sands

I have heard that in Morocco the sands sing.
Like tiny beads sorted, the constant secret
shuffle of the living song sung in the moving grain.

What great instrument the winds bring
to the funneled sands. Little alphabet
of scales as the Morocco sands sink and sing.

I wish to lie in the wild dunes listening
to the sands that know how to let
the shifts of song sing in the moving grain.

The sands of China do not have the same ring
as the sands of Morocco. The sun has set
and now the drifting tunnel of grit sings

the opening notes in the dry sting
of sands sorted. Always the great unrest lets
the voice stay alive in the surge of the moving grain.

Desert songs the ancients, too, heard sing.
Each avalanche lies disquieted, that we not forget
to hear the Moroccan sands sing:
a voice alive and the song sung in the moving grain.

Echo

This blond god the stemmed narcissus
is a stunning centerpiece if you like the dead;
how still the flowers sit in rigor mortis
with no great diffidence for the grave.

If you like the dead

the drowned are charming and no longer shun
the living. To die for lack of the water's kiss,
image touched to image, and the pun
of my echo still unwon by him.

The water's kiss

will not relieve him and he no longer wants to live
except for the strong blond god the water shows,
and how the water lets go, the god in the sieve
of his hands runs dry.

What the water shows

we both could love. And yet I am still in the meadow
and he is only bones in the fountain.

Here. Here. In the meadow.

Daphne

Let the crow shelter in my shadow.
I live in the seam of the tree where the wild blossom grows.
Lightning and soot!—my heart is heartwood now.
Only my taproot knows how far down I go.

I am moss and death on my south side.
My pulse the vein of the leaf.
Stilled solitude of the suicide,
I hold the quelled breath

shunted in the quiet shoot.
I am mute metamorphosis!
Each eye, shut, is my own blind fruit.
I am ruin and stasis like Isis

holding the dead in her wings.
Spilled silent sap—the wood sings!

Persephone Writes Home

1.
Mother, what if my heart is an aviary
instead of an arbor? What if my heart
is all birds instead of roses? Migratory
the cages of wings instead of petals. We part,

Mother, like the moon and its orbit: I am a stolen
piece of your light. Petals jilted
from the rose, and all the swollen
spring left in great troughs of winter wilted.

It is always evening here; in the mauve
dark I wish for more than the white
winged moths. Night's hands like your kidskin glove!
My heart an aviary where I can't take flight.

The sky is a bleak and holy trousseau:
among shadows I, too, rise indigo.

2.
Mother, my mouth still quivers with the blood
of this fruit: crimson seeds palmed
in his hand. The lilies and monkshood
he ripped from my arms. How calm

the pomegranate's glassy seeds
on my tongue. Are you in the fields now,
your straw hat shielding your eyes, and the weeds
cut down by your firm hand on the plow?

I wear veils of dust, and I wonder what you
are singing to yourself among the wheat,
humming, inspecting stalk tips. How new
the dead are to me, and how old is the fruit's deceit.

Mother, you did not tell me not to cut my hair;
now my hair is like ashes spread out from an old fire.

3.
Rust colors the pomegranate rind.
I cannot touch the corpse's perfumed hand.
The dead fall carelessly like a woman's pins
strewn from loosened hair. In Asian sands

the pomegranate grows. The dark is feminine,
in that a daughter is her mother's shadow.
In the fruit's red skin are six seeds of sin.
Here every shadow casts a shadow.

As in a groove the hooves move
the horses in the grove of hell—
but it is their wild manes I love.
The moon does not rise or set in hell.

Here, survivors of a city ruined
carry their unworldly, beautiful wounds.

Part Three

Mirror

Tainted with smoke as she braided her hair before the mirror,
Mother's hands held the reflected tangle of smoke and braid
in the mirror, too. When had Mother begun to smoke and Father

stopped? Father tamped and let the little ember
breathe like a part of him afire. Self-made,
they said of Father. Silent in smoke Mother looked to her mirror.

Father and Mother were slowly changing one into the other,
she in her riding vest and the length of her hair a braid
in a red ribbon; and the little lit heart of Father

acquitted and lent to Mother. A matching red ribbon Mother
gave to the mane of her horse. We watched the red fade
out of the ribbons as Mother did her hair in the mirror.

Slim spiral smoke the sibyl sings as arbiter
of love; once Mother kissed Uncle and Father forbade
the weaving of the ribbon. The mirror held smoke and Father:

when had Father begun to smoke and Mother
stopped? Without Mother, Uncle took off with the maid.
Tainted with smoke Mother braided her hair before the mirror.
In the mirror, Mother's lips kissed the brier pipe instead of Father.

Horoscope

In a salon of blood, in the sea's gall,
in a parlor chair where only the cat sits,
inside a forge, seams of bell
solder-rung: my one consummate cell,
drowned Narcissus in a mirrored hall,
divides, divides love's requisites;
I the startle-eyed nuclei my mother will expel
from the out-of-season room let in the womb's hotel.

It is boring in the womb,
where are dunes of fanned-out magazines on tables in a waiting
    room?
Blood-bound vein-reined
we conduct through aqueduct:
cord that is the mother that is the love that is all other loves.
In buoyant climes I beat webbed fists, while she ungloves,
placing cold-turning papers, news before
us: I will know my horoscope and the weather in Baltimore;

that stars align trajectories of bullet and flower;
that in sips of amniotic fluid we love what we devour.

Gray Day

I have come from some vague place of her,
slumber of her thighs easing me out:
I am the raw color of bologna, cocksure
and upside-down to the world in my blood and my shout,

and free of our pact, free of her waters
where I neither drowned nor breathed.
Like the swan with its cygnet she is with her daughters,
protecting us from some grave unknown foe. I teethed

on her nipples, I scarred her aureole
until she fed me biscuits and whey.
Now her long silk wedding gloves fit the whole
length of my arms—and on a gray

day I wed him—I in her white gloves
danced with her bare arms on me, she the only one I'd ever loved.

Mother

She is the cord cut clean.
She is blood made into blood.
She is the navel's scar and seam.
She is love misunderstood.

She is the navel's shroud of skin
marred, mended, severed, saved.
She is not the Mary Magdalene.
She is not all goodness or the goddess in her cave.

She is not the largess of breasts unburied
of the Willendorf Venus. She has no snakes
like Medusa in her hair. The need
to release us from our first mirroring of her makes

her great: she has given us the larger world
just as we have realized she is not our only world.

Mammato-Cumulus

Mammato-cumulus: hanging, breast-like
protuberances on the undersurface of a cloud.

Was the first woman made of clay or cloud?
Changeling of wind and rain, shape-shifter,
even Zeus came to his lover Io in the guise of a cloud.
Cold mother of udder and vapor,

drifter enclosing the microscopic grit
the raindrop carries within it,
who can measure your gait
across the sky, and your teats

that sometimes coalesce and sometimes evaporate?
How lewd, how ancient, the cloud-crone
who carries at times the shriveled aggregate
of a dozen breasts like a beast's litter of fed demons.

Above, the clouds are cold as the jade's whorl.
Below, weaned at great loss, is the jaded world.

Ghost

The ghost, or cognate, is a paler second or third print pulled from the original printing plate that has been inked only once.

Turning, turning, the great wheels
of her press, my mother makes the lighter twin
scavenged from its brighter double. Twin steals
from twin: mute doppelgänger as the wheel spins

silent, stops. The returning image dies
twice before it dies. My mother's eyes
are my eyes one shade darker. What dries
on the paper is a little vitae

of our qualities: I am my mother once diluted.
The nose, the lips, the caresses, and the creases
of her grace I inherit; all else I've looted.
I am like a silvery fish too small that she releases.

Turning, turning, the wheels cannot stop the ghost:
wondrous colors' waste—I am the ink ever-lost!

Obiter Dicta

I follow my mother's orbit day
by day; it's her hands that my hands betray.
Her obit is mine—words' silver-stilled set gray!
Her cursive hand relays me back to her recursive clay.

Each cursive letter once precise and small, now stalls to sway.
Posted envelopes, ounce by ounce, she weighs.
(As an infant she sat me on the ancient scale's cracked tray!)
Marks scraped on a prisoner's wall: her face tallies

wrinkles, divined surely as the artist who lays
copper plate to mordant bath. Atheist, she cannot pray;
she finds the gods passé, and prefers Monet on Sundays.
Her hands are ghostly-burdened anyway.

I am the loom—she makes the weave and dye of me—
begged vanished threads from Penelope!

Wedding Portrait

Against the photographer's drapes of trompe l'oeil scenes,
Father and Mother stood between Egypt and the Red Sea.
Behind Mother, the promise of quince and cypress trees.

Behind Father, the hidden aloes planted by some queen
are drawn upon the screen. Beside Mother the ebony
trees painted on the drapes' trompe l'oeil scenes.

They stand against the gardens of Babylon to convene
their marriage among the false silent sea
and the brushstrokes of cypress trees.

To love the broken gods might be blasphemy.
Before the lost columns and the ivory
inlaid god, against the drapes' trompe l'oeil scenes,

Mother and Father fit into the scheme:
olives and Zeus and the hot sands of the sea.
Behind Mother, the promise of quince and cypress trees.

Shutter-caught shining stone eyes gleamed
on Olympia: a tower, a statue, a colossus, and Mother's green
eyes against the drapes' trompe l'oeil scenes.
Behind Mother, the promise of quince and cypress trees.

Chess

There are always papers on Father's desk.
Slowly he lifts one sheet out of the chaos.
On the top ledge of the roll-top desk sits the chess
board. He has taught me the moves of the rook and the horse.

Slowly the papers of insurance and indemnity
are each lifted in turn and held to the midnight
light. My queen is white and his queen is ebony.
High on the desktop his knight faces my knight.

I try to copy his signature where the letters'
loops fall like slow lassoes that drag in dust.
The receipts are fettered to a spike. The debtor
in January adjusts the bills of August.

I hear my mother turn and the bedspring
slowly creak. My father sits facing the impotent ebony king.

Leaf

Once Father put a fall leaf into his Keats
and closed the book. The leaf faded to lace
the color of tea. Father still felt regret
for a woman loved before Mother. Even Mother's waist,

slender and strong, couldn't erase thoughts
of the other. Thirty years later
he saw her again. A scarf tied in a knot
covered her cancer scar. Her voice was gone, only a purr

in its place. Once it was easy to believe in beauty
and truth and to read Keats until midnight.
Wasn't it God's duty to keep truth and beauty
like the scales of the stars of Libra? Who to indict?

Father opened the page to the rot of the leaf.
His hoarse cry as his grief met Keats's grief.

Handkerchief

Father had angina, and a locket like a metal bullet
laced around his neck, holding nitroglycerin.
In war he'd killed a man with his bayonet.
Now Father's heart's blood blew like a sea wind

through a draft of valves and veins.
He held his secret second breath in the silver vial
that kept him going. In the mud and the rain
he had stolen the handkerchief while

the man he'd speared sputtered sputum.
Some ancient threaded initial, *V,* or *W,*
was embroidered on the cotton; a strange perfume,
flowers tempered with blood, left a residue

on the folded cloth. Father said he closed the dead man's
eyes: green, like Father's, like faded jade or celadon.

Honeymoon

Father and Mother went to a dude ranch for their honeymoon.
Father's shirts had pearlized buttons
and Mother wore gaucho pants. Roses strewn
on the bed sheets, and Father's handgun

hidden in the nightstand drawer
next to Mother's lace and satin lingerie.
One day Mother's horse threw her.
Mother was put in a wheelchair, and the bay

horse led back to the stalls.
They had been married twelve days.
The doctor said that Mother, after the fall,
might not have babies. The wild red roses dried to gray

and were swept from the bed. Father put down the bay with his gun.
Like Eve out of clay and torn bone Mother bore her children.

Son

That lost son, born before my sister
and I, was hardly more than a bundle
of blood, mucous, feces, and death, the listed
prow of a drowned vessel. The herbs the pestle

crushed were not enough to ensure life for him,
but Mother ground and ate the nettles anyway.
There is no arithmetic for that unbalanced sum,
the son born, but not quite born, one cloudy day.

He had a name, he had a cry, and hair
already coming in. But in his cry
he was polite and quieted in their arms. The glare
of the doctor's lights focused in each eye

and death came on between the seeing and the blink.
Carefully the nurses washed his dead body at the sink.

Gift

Soul to kindred soul kindled
between the fox and the woman.
Gleaned of backbone and knuckle,
the fox's ersatz eye cut like the polish of cabochon.

Mother's gaze too seemed made of glazed glass.
Under the thick furl of her false eyelashes
Mother hardly blinked, caught in the brass-
flecked foundry of her banded irises. As if in whiplash

the fox collar's cradled slender snout wrapped
round at the sweater's neckline. The grace
was taken out with the backbone. The nape
of fur bore the burned spot of ember and ash at the place

where her cigarette singed the fur. Like a sibyl of Babylon,
the fox's stony eye was the last gift, then Father was gone.

My Father's World

My father's desk was his world,
the tiger-grain lost beneath the varnish and the darkened wax,
and in the drawers a wilderness harnessed to the ordered world.

My mother had no desk, just a chair where she could knit and purl,
while my father sat and calculated his toil and tax.
My father's desk was his world.

At his touch and pull, a little panel unfurled
to form an adjacent writing space for me, next to where his cognac
sat. A wilderness harnessed to the ordered world,

he filled the drawers with fountain pens marbled
in mock tortoise shell; like honey in combed wax,
a bottle's mucilage. My father's desk was his world.

I was not like every other girl:
instead of dolls I preferred my father's graphite pencils and his stacks
of unread mail that threatened the order of his world.

In the underbelly of the varnished wood was a whorl
of shellac I stroked. Mother's needles creaked and clacked like the
cracking
of some other world that belonged only to her. My father's desk was
his world.
Order and chaos and the tiger-stripe: I entered my father's world.

Part Four

Birds of the New World

Death's lilting sleep recalls the voyage out
of Puerto Rico, towards Virginia, where fifteen
men in 1586 were left to found a colony. About
the flamingo's tongue: it lay between

the sacred and the profane—a delicacy the Romans ate;
but what can one say of the graceful bones
of fifteen men scattered among melons and deer? We annotate
the past and write the preface of the future to disown

the linear world; yet, like the lopsided noise
of the woodpecker, we search out death
in the tall trees, where like choirboys,
the towhee and the merganser, sing. What stealth,

this new world, where the birds fall and fly like Icarus—
and the deadly sleep of fifteen men under perfect cirrus.

Icarus

Half-breed of the air I fly feather to flame,
wing to wave and the king's maze below me.
The sea is my homecoming. I am my father's fame,
for who would remember him without me?

A father ties his son's wings and sends him skyborne.
The ocean's open grave is mother to me. Wax worn
on my back and the warning of the foghorn
as I plummet down with only Father to mourn

me. Father, saved, hangs his wings on a hook.
The sun that took his son is blameless.
It was my own unmaking for I had to look
into the terrible eye of the star. Shameless

Lorelei drags me under and I lie in her arms.
My melted wings death gently disarms.

Woman with Wing Removed

The angels have left me, the birds have not found me,
the surgeon has sealed the seam.
I cannot say the wing made me free,
or that I flew in my dreams

higher than the painted brides of Chagall. I cannot say
I ever flew, or that it wasn't the vestige
of primordial form that an artist pinches up from the clay.
If the ribs are a cage, it wasn't a cage;

it seemed like a place for the wind,
a place to keep the thunder and rain.
One lone feather settles on my spine
drifting down from the sterile air. No one can explain

the excised wing, velvet and veined as leaved milkweed.
Now where will the thunder breed?

Thunder

Love, do you know, I've hung a bell
on every knob of every door to not miss
you; the chime I'll hear will foretell
your entrance or your leaving. Let the clapper kiss

the bronze to toll our visits. How still
our lips, how quiet flesh finds flesh:
the bells ring recklessly against the skill
to make our clamor silent—even the thrush

sings sometimes soft and sometimes loud
and weaves her nest for her lover, just as I knot
the ribbon through the bell to shake a little cloud
of thunder as it gives out to the pressure of your knock.

Darling, the doors are unlocked and ringing, yet I am in doubt—
how is it I cannot tell if you are coming in or going out?

Ginger

How is it my lover's lips taste of ginger?
The taste of ginger does not come easily.
Coaxed out of the tiny jar, the curry lingers
on the breath—but this is not the season

for heat or curry—these are days of mud
held between the great divides of rain and snow
that brings on spring between the sudden
rutting of the buck and the budding of the willow.

I tuck a blossom of white ginger
into my hair—the flower has withstood the arctic florist ice,
stolen from some tropic lair—my clever fingers
braid it to my hair. This is not the season for spice

but all the same my lover's lips swell with ginger.
I touch the flower in my hair—I too cannot wreck the spell of ginger.

Apple

Tiny poisonous eyes' salt and cyanide:
onyx seeds, glance of stone
recanting out of dulcet flesh.

Grafts, vinegar, and fire blight:
the orchard's limbs archaic as Rome;
spellbound spheres of gold: apples for Atalanta.

Adam knew dawn, Eve knew dusk;
Adam born the first hour of day, Eve the seventh:
mother offered the night fruit to father.

Footprint baren-and-dabber inked in midnight light
of morgue and birthing room;
blossom-rust of aphid, moth: in the twelfth hour, expelled—

who to winter-prune the sweet-fleshed fruit sour-sung to wine?

Apples

The apples are bitter, the orchard haphazard.
Half-eaten blackened cores lie like bones in a graveyard.
No one to prune the trees and the fruit frozen.
Brutal and tortured, the snowy limbs bend.
In the ice the sour fruit glitters.
                    The apples are bitter.

Winter bees feed in the glassed honeycomb.
Dead wasps have abandoned their paper dome home.
Once Adam had the word and Eve had the apple,
then the snake gave free will to the first couple.
The edge of the orchard and the edge of paradise are bitter—
                    just so, these apples, too, are bitter.

Vase

I have let all the apples fall to the ground.
The white blossoms are gone, and the moths
have scattered out of their cocoons soundlessly.
Summer, and I am thirsty as the animals at their trough.

The apples started as fists, tiny and green,
but now they cannot keep hold on the branches.
Spellbound, the spilled apples are like some green
jade or beryl marred. My face blanches

without make-up, pale as moth wings.
The apples are twisted and misshapen.
What should I do with the vessel you gave me—a Ming
vase that also has moths, painted in the glaze? When

are you coming back?—the fruit is fallen and the tree is bare.
Found in formed flames of the vase, on one moth's wing, is a scar.

Vessel

To be colored in metallic salt,
dipped in cobalt
blue, raku's
flame-tamed hues
equatorial smoke and wintry water.

To reside in luster:
illicit god's chamber-
quarantined gold.
To be the stone—small, in blindfold,
pressed to the vessel's

burnished sides. To be the pestle's
love against the mortar:
plot of glaze, guise of feldspar.
To be the shard-skin:
glass cast-out of manganese, iron, livid tin.

To be the callow body
vitrified in journey
near catastrophe:
something new arises out of desire
of water, earth and furtive-fettered fire.

Fire and Flux

The miry-drenched wooden rib
to sleek and articulate the shoulders
and neck of the pot:

turning tools incised upon the body,
cured in fire and flux,
chemist-crackled colors;

upon the whirling wheel
turned, pulled, trimmed,
liquid-glazed kiln-banished:

like Eve placed beside the cassia-bark tree,
the potter's voice never again
among the resined branches.

Veined-Garden

Before he was pure, Adam was impure.
Birth-bed silt,
he and Lilith a muddy pair,
each given a tail, some said.

Lilith came out of dust, Eve out of bone.
Holding the ivory rib, cupping the handful of dirt:
God satiated in unspeakable name
as others were on remnants of jewel-red fruit.

Before Eve was impure, she was pure.
Eve with no mother but the cold-boned rib.
Skin of the apple, sweet compote in her teeth,
red as the heart's hibiscus-colored veined-garden.

I in Eden Born

After I was born, a nurse held up a mirror
for my mother's reds of lips and rouge:
in the mirror, my mother saw Eve collecting
gems, onyx, and gold in the forked rivers of Eden.

Somewhere in Eden, did Eve lift a mirror
and see my mother, gatherer of earthly roots and moss,
seed-pods and stones river-rushed?

Glassed among what leafy specimen,
what gnarled thing precious to my mother,
was I in Eden born?

Pomegranate

The stub of the stem juts
out of its severed joint. The gelid seeds
spliced between pith and pit. Halved orb cut
clean as the brain's hemispheres! The tacit need

to be held at knifepoint.
This husk did not havoc harm
in the coming out of Eden. Persephone, hell's housewife,
packed her bag and toiletries by March. Who warned

Eve that she had no mother but the abstract
rib? What myths—Venus is a relic
shawled in shell and the snake is only artifact.
Bright lobes and blood-red seeds, opened disc

held on the flat palm of Dis.
As she sipped the seeds she felt the kiss of all of Hades.

Persephone

A midrash tells us that the pomegranate contains 613 seeds, the number of mitzvoth (commandments) found in the Torah.

First she missed the lilies and the violets.
Then she was in love with Hades' hazel eye.
Those six seeds lent her were her debt.
Hell's green eye lit like the glassed firefly.

Half-caste of heaven and hell, stillborn
stale waters ferried her over.
Hangover of too-much mother scything the corn.
Borne down the river Styx, she was ready for a lover.

She brought back to hell lilies in a vase—
come winter, the leaves and flowers were marred
and dead. Wed, she had spider webs instead of lace.
Spring and fall, coins for Charon and passage in and out of the
     graveyard.

She's heard another god has fixed all sin:
613 commandments—like the hail of seeds thrown against the wind!

Hepatica

Does Persephone know, that out of rifts of snow,
the hepatica blooms in February?
To chop at the frozen ground with the claw of the hoe,
this is Demeter's way, solitary in her sanctuary.

The moths and the bees will know this flower
that blooms too soon for Persephone still under
her trek of hell. Hell has no off-hour,
like the neon lights of storefronts, comes the wonder

of the too-bright lights in the still-dark morning.
Once mother and daughter watched the purple flowers together.
How strange it is that death is boring—and spring's mourning
insincere before the lightning storms of summer.

The cold plaster sets the death mask,
while still the face is for the living's task.

Hecate

Because she stands at the crossroads,
she can look into the past, present, and future.

Full moon: the too-large pupil's doctored drops
dilated in the waiting room, and soon the chart
projected, scrolled, all the little props
of blindness tolled, as seeing is an art

the same as other guilds and must be learned
like the blacksmith's fire or the gilder's gold.
The kohled eye watery and cold, sojourns
a little orbit and sees on the threshold

of the brain. But the moon is old, old,
and has a dressing room of clothes too small,
too big; waning, waxing, the story is retold
by ancient Hecate who can still recall

how once she was a child born in bloody fur: messenger
still tethered between the midwife and the mother.

Dust out of Eden

Endless dust as out of ancient cities
of Syria and Sodom: all the dust
of Genesis rides this freighter. Dust out of Eden:

dust of the Tigress below; and above the Pleiades.
Flatbed cars hold the hog's last breath, and the dung
of cattle. Endless dust of ancient cities,

and the blood of the chicken and the grease
of lambs' wool. Coal and sulfur, ashes and slag rolling under Sirius.
Trains pulling Cain's grain and sorghum. Out of Eden

the dust of the Nile. Coffee, sugar, and tea
held in the bashed doors of the *Santa Fe.* Rust
of the *Union,* the *Baltimore and Ohio.* Ancient cities

like the mobile spine of the *Sooline's* soliloquies
turned in the switching yard. Thrust
of the hopper of Genesis; riding the dust out of Eden.

In porcelain and glass and aluminum the milk going east.
Blood point of the eggshell cradled in straw. Exodus
is all. Dust of apples, potatoes; dust out of ancient cities.
Mourners and murderers: all the dust of Genesis rides this train out
    of Eden.

Agave

Time has won the flower. How odd
the bloom foretells death's hour. What god
would let time kill the plant to win
the flower? After fifty years the first bloom begins,
one bloom that tolls death's hour.
                    Time has won the flower.

Useless now, the succulent leaves and their spines;
all, all now is the flower's shrine
in the slow death foretold in the bloom.
The agave is dying in its glassed conservatory room.
After fifty years the rosette lets the stalk flower.
                    Time has won the flower.

Hawk

Wild the need to leave the cage of love!
Love for the living and love for the dead, balanced on the fisted glove.
Forced love over earned love.
Under the blinding the hawk still wants the moor. Above,

shadowed hood made of calf skin; below,
knot and tie of the hawk's leg. Above,
the trimmed beak sharpened speechless. Slow
is the master's throwing arm; slow the love

of the prey of little mammals mouthed: mice, pigeon,
hare, and quail—what little harm
to eat the bones, flesh, claws, teeth, and feathers. Harlequin's
harsh-tuned bells at anklet tied by the alien arm

that favors forced loyalty over sporadic love.
Wild the need to leave the cage of love!

About the Author

Valerie Wohlfeld's first collection, *Thinking the World Visible*, was chosen by James Dickey for the Yale Series of Younger Poets Prize. While writing that book, she lived in a three-hundred-year-old house in Massachusetts; she has continued to live in New England for more than two decades. She received a master of fine arts in writing from Vermont College. Published widely, her poems have appeared in *The New Yorker*, *The Yale Review*, *Poetry*, *Antioch Review*, *New England Review*, *The Hopkins Review*, and elsewhere.